This Book is a Gift

To

From

On the Occasion of

Date

DREAM BIG & SUCCEED

Proven Nuggets For Successful Achievement

SUNDAY A. EZEKIEL

Dream Big & Succeed
Copyright © 2017 by:
Sunday A. Ezekiel

ISBN: 978-171-863-662-0

Published in Nigeria by:
DW-Impact Ltd, Lagos – Nigeria

All rights reserved. No portion of this publication may be reproduced, stored in retrieval system, or transmitted in any form by any means – electronic, mechanical, photocopying, recording, or any other – without the prior written permission of the publisher, except for brief quotations in printed reviews, magazines, articles etc.

For further enquiries, distribution or permission, contact:

Dreamers World Christian Centre

Phone:
+234-8035122385, +234-7082982341

Email:
info@dreamersworldng.org

CONTENT

INTRODUCTION	vii
CHAPTER 1 - THE POWER OF POSITIVE DREAMS	01
CHAPTER 2 - YOUR DREAM IS YOUR AREA OF INFLUENCE	03
CHAPTER 3 - YOUR INNER WORLD CREATES YOUR OUTER WORLD	05
CHAPTER 4 - YOUR DREAM COMES THROUGH INSIGHT & FORESIGHT	07
CHAPTER 5 - WRITE DOWN YOUR DREAM AGAIN	09
CHAPTER 6 - YOUR REASON FOR LIVING	11
CHAPTER 7 - YOUR IMAGINATION FORMS YOUR DREAM	13
CHAPTER 8 - UNDERSTANDING THE POWER OF IDEAS	15
CHAPTER 9 - UNDERSTANDING THE POWER OF PURPOSE	17
CHAPTER 10 - UNLEASH YOUR POTENTIAL	19
CHAPTER 11 - YOU CAN ACHIEVE MORE THAN YOU HAVE	21
CHAPTER 12 - YOUR ATTITUDE DETERMINE YOUR ALTITUDE	23
CHAPTER 13 - YOUR DREAM IS TO SERVE PEOPLE	25
CHAPTER 14 - YOU CAN FAIL FORWARD TO ACHIEVE YOUR DREAM	27
CHAPTER 15 - TURNING YOUR PAINS TO PROGRESS & YOUR SETBACKS TO SUCCESS	29
CHAPTER 16 - AWAKEN THE BIG DREAM WITHIN YOU	31
CHAPTER 17 - BE INNOVATIVE IN YOUR THINKING	33
CHAPTER 18 - BUILD YOUR DREAM TEAM	35
CHAPTER 19 - CELEBRATE THE REALITY OF YOUR BIG DREAM	37
CHAPTER 20 - CHANGE YOUR THINKING, CHANGE YOUR LIFE	39
CHAPTER 21 - CREATING THE ACTUAL PICTURES OF YOUR DREAM	41
CHAPTER 22 - CREATIVE THINKING DIMENSION	43
CHAPTER 23 - DARE YOUR DREAM	45

CHAPTER 24 - DECIDE WHAT YOU WANT	47
CHAPTER 25 - DETERMINE TO WIN	49
CHAPTER 26 - DISCOVER YOUR PURPOSE	51
CHAPTER 27 - DO YOU HAVE A MISSION STATEMENT?	53
CHAPTER 28 - DREAMERS ARE COMMITTED LEARNERS	55
CHAPTER 29 - DREAMERS ARE LEADERS WITH A DARING SPIRIT	57
CHAPTER 30 - EXPECTATION: YOUR WINNING KEY	59
CHAPTER 31 - FOCUS ON YOUR DREAM	61
CHAPTER 32 - GREAT ACHIEVERS ARE GOALS ORIENTED	63
CHAPTER 33 - IF YOU CAN SEE IT, YOU CAN GET IT	65
CHAPTER 34 - IMPROVE YOURSELF TO FULFIL YOUR DREAM	67
CHAPTER 35 - MASTER YOUR MIND TO ACHIEVE YOUR DREAM	69
CHAPTER 36 - NEVER GIVE UP ON YOUR DREAM	71
CHAPTER 37 - PAY THE PRICE FOR YOUR DREAM	73
CHAPTER 38 - PLAN TO FULFIL YOUR DREAM	75
CHAPTER 39 - PRESS ON WITH FOCUS	77
CHAPTER 40 - PROBLEMS ARE YOUR OPPORTUNITIES FOR PROGRESS	79
CHAPTER 41 - PURSUE YOUR DREAM	81
CHAPTER 42 - PURSUE YOUR DREAM WITH PASSION	83
CHAPTER 43 - P.U.S.H FOR YOUR DREAM	85
CHAPTER 44 - REFUSE TO QUIT ON YOUR DREAM	87
CHAPTER 45 - RELEASING YOUR POTENTIAL	89
CHAPTER 46 - SET GOALS FOR YOUR DREAM	91
CHAPTER 47 - SPEAK YOUR DREAM INTO REALITY	93
CHAPTER 48 - STAND OUT & FULFILL YOUR DREAM	95
CHAPTER 49 - STOP PROCRASTINATING: ACT NOW!	97
CHAPTER 50 - STUMBLING BLOCKS ARE YOUR STEPPING STONES	99
CHAPTER 51 - SUCCESS IS IN YOU; BRING IT OUT!	101
CHAPTER 52 - THE POWER OF ASSOCIATION	103
CHAPTER 53 - THE VIRTUE OF PATIENCE	105

Introduction

> *"Success is achieved when a stretch goal is met overcoming failures, problems and difficulties by conscious effort and by application of capabilities, resources and*

Success is not a cheap talk; rather, it places a great demand on anyone who desires to have it. Also, success is not a destination; rather, it is a journey. Additionally success is in grades and levels and it has different colours depending individual's perception.

Dreams are seeds of great accomplishments and fulfillment in life. Success in every endeavour of man is traceable to the dream of man. To put it in another way; no man can fulfill a divine mandate without engaging the power of dream. In other words, the reason for failure in the race of life is a direct product of lack of dream. Dreams are extremely important, because, you cannot do anything successfully unless you can imagine it first. In order to succeed, man must first determine which things in life are most valuable to him. He must determine his feeling about such things as patriotism, pride, love, freedom, excellence, ownership and tolerance. Without a value system we can never move forward, because, we may be trading without increasing our potential for success. Our value system is what determines our thinking and dream patterns.

In this book, I am going to be exploring some of the various aspects of the subject of success through your dream for the purpose of sparking off the passion for success in you.

Each chapter contains short words of motivation that will drive you into your success dreamland.

Welcome to your season of great achievement as you

CHAPTER 1: THE POWER OF POSITIVE DREAMS

> *"Thought is the fountain of action, life and manifestation; make the fountain pure, and all will be pure. All that man achieves and all that he fails to achieve is the direct result of his thoughts. As he thinks, so he is, as he continues to think, so he remains".*
> **James Allen**

*D*reams are created through the process of thinking. When you take the time to engage in long term positive thinking, you in the process of creating positive events which becomes your dream.

I read a story about when Bill Gates was still a very young chap living with his parents. One day his mother was looking for him, shouting "Bill, Bill, where are you?"

After a long time of searching for him in the house, she open a door in one of the rooms in the house and found in sitting down alone. Then she asked, "What are you doing here alone?" Bill answered, "**I am Thinking. Don't you think**?"

Today, we can see the result of those early years of positive thinking of Bill Gates. It was out of those thoughts that the BIG DREAM called MICROSOFT INC. came out.

Friend, your positive thinking of today is your dream that will create a future for you. Therefore, **THINK BIG, THINK POSITIVE and SUCCEED.**

CHAPTER 2: YOUR DREAM IS YOUR AREA OF INFLUENCE

> *"All successful people, men and women are big dreamers. They imagine what their future could be, ideal in every respect, and then they work every day toward their distant vision, goal or purpose."*
> **Brian Tracy**

The birth of a great dreamer, Michael Faraday is a great blessing to mankind as a result of the reality of his dream of electricity as a solution to the world of darkness.

The world will never recover from the great dream of Thomas Edison which became a reality in form of the incandescent light bulb after trying to get it done for more than a thousand times.

The great dreamer; Alexander Graham Bell turned his dream of easy communication over a long distance to reality through his invention of the telephone.

Isaac Newton; the inventor of the Law of Gravity provided a solution in global scientific development through the reality of his dream.

The best time to begin is now. Therefore, **DREAM BIG and SUCCEED**

CHAPTER 3: YOUR INNER WORLD CREATES YOUR OUTER WORLD

"Thoughts and ideas are the source of all wealth, success, material gain, all great discoveries, inventions and achievements"
Mark Victor Hansen

Everything we produce on the outside are direct products of who we are on the inside. We can therefore conclude that the heart of the matter is a matter of the heart.

You cannot really feature in a future that you have not actually pictured. What you are within is what you produce without.

Your physical realities are direct print out of the soft copy of your inner thoughts. To change your material realities you must change the information in the source from where they are produced.

As a man thinketh…..so is he, as he continues to think…..so he remain.

It is what you keep putting in and processing within that determines what you will keep getting without. Change the information in the source by DREAMING BIG and you will produce the result of your BIG DREAM.

IT IS YOUR INNER WORLD THAT CREATES YOUR OUTER WORLD.

I challenge you today to **DREAM BIG and SUCCEED.**

CHAPTER 4: YOUR DREAM COMES THROUGH INSIGHT & FORESIGHT

"If you can imagine it, you can achieve it. If you can dream it, you can become it".
William Arthur Ward

Insight is the ability to see into the depth of a situation. It is synonymous with intuition which means inner teacher and it also means perspective. Insight is a combination of experience, reasoning, views and sensitivity to the voice of your inner man within you. You have to listen to the voice within. You have to learn how to turn down the volume of the voice outside and turn on the volume of the voice of your inner man. This voice tells you who you are and what can happen in your life.

Foresight on the other hand is the ability to see into the future. It is about where you are going; your destination and your determination to get there.

Foresight is the ability to see what has not happened in your mind and being ready to create them in the physical realm. That is exactly what dream or vision is. To have foresight is to have a dream or vision. Foresight is the type of sight that helps you see way down the road and believe in the possibility of a great future.

You must have both insight and foresight and be able to combine the two to form a dream and then you must believe in the possibility of your dream. Insight mixed with foresight gives you the key for tapping into the power of dream for exploits.

Therefore, friend, **DREAM BIG and SUCCEED**

CHAPTER 5: WRITE DOWN YOUR DREAM AGAIN

> *"I would like to repeat the critical importance of committing your plan to writing. It cannot be overemphasized!"*
> **Paul J. Meyer**

Documenting your dream in details has power to transform your life. Until you are able to document your dream in detail, using sentences, graphs, charts, or pictures, you cannot fully realize its object.

I have discovered that there is a great power in writing down what you want to do before you begin. That is why you must take the time to do series of writings, drawings and plotting your dream in a very clear term.

According to a research study carried out by Harvard University few years ago, it was discovered that ninety-five percent of the things you write down come to pass. As soon as you put your dream of paper, it takes on the power of itself.

Writing your dream is not a one time exercise; it is a lifetime issues. This is because the fullness of dream may not be released all at once.

The dream you do not write down in detail, its object you may not achieve. And no matter how sharp you think your memory is, you cannot fulfill a dream that is not well well written down. Someone once said, "The shortest pencil is sharper than the sharpest brain."

Have you taken the time to write down your dream? Do you have a book you can call "MY DREAM BOOK?"

I challenge you today to **DREAM BIG, WRITE DOWN YOUR DREAM and SUCCEED.**

CHAPTER 6: YOUR REASON FOR LIVING

> *"Human beings are capable of incredible things. If we have a big enough REASON to do something, we'll go to the greatest lengths to get it done."*
> **Anthony Robbins**

Having a dream is having a reason for living. Anyone without a dream is just existing rather than living.

But without a knowledge of your identity, you will lack the knowledge of your purpose. Your identity is who you are, your purpose is why you are alive.

You need to understand that, there is nothing as important in your life as your mental attitude towards yourself - what you think of yourself, the model which you hold of yourself and your possibilities.

It is the knowledge of who you are that dictates your mental attitude toward yourself and that mental attitude will dictate how you relate with your creator who is the source of your purpose.

The major truth of life is that, you can not be truly successful until you truly know yourself. It is the knowledge of 'who' you are that lends credence to the knowledge of 'why' you are.

If you truly desire to succeed, you need to discover your true identity and the reason why you are alive. Your dream will have its root in this knowledge.

It is never late to get it right. And the best time to begin is NOW. DREAM BIG through a discovery of your identity and your reason for living and **YOU WILL SUCCEED**

CHAPTER 7: YOUR IMAGINATION FORMS YOUR DREAM

"Having a dream is not trying to believe something regardless of the evidence, dreaming is daring to do something regardless of the consequences. Let your faith run ahead of your mind."
John Mason

Imagination is the ability to form a mental image of something that is not perceived through the senses. It is the ability of the mind to build mental scenes, objects or events that do not exist, are not present or have happened in the past.

Memory is actually a manifestation of imagination. Everyone possesses some imagination ability. In some it may be highly developed and in others it may manifest in a weaker form. It manifests in various degrees in various people.

Imagination makes it possible to experience a whole world inside the mind. It gives the ability to look at any situation from a different point of view, and enables one to mentally explore the past and the future.

You need to understand that it will be impossible for you to feature in a future that you have not pictured, because it is your mental picture that forms the basis for the actualization of your actual future.

Genevieve Behrend said; "Try to remember that the picture you think, feel and see is reflected into the Universal Mind, and by the natural law of reciprocal action must return to you in either spiritual or physical form."

This means pictures are formed by your imagination and this eventually transforms into your dream in real life.

DREAM BIG through your **IMAGINATION and SUCCEED**

CHAPTER 8: UNDERSTANDING THE POWER OF IDEAS

"Ideas have enormous power, since they form the frame of our understanding of the world, inform our beliefs and drive our behaviours. Great ideas are so profound and frame-shaking that they quickly topple many of the things we believe, and transform our worldviews, our values and hence our actions. We need more great ideas, and a deeper understanding of how and when they transform our understanding, our culture, what we do and who we are."
Dave Pollard

Ideas are extremely powerful force that engage people's minds and help them see new possibilities and new opportunities. Strong and evocative ideas energize people and incite action.

Our productivity is what determines our level of influence on the earth; and the minimum requirement for achievement is just an idea. A great future awaits all of us, but that future is waiting for the thoughts God wants to transfer into our minds Ideas are more powerful than the brains that produce them because the usually outlive those brains. Ideas mean thoughts, plans or mental impression on the mind.

Creation begins with an idea. Since God built us in His image, He has made us with the capacity to produce thoughts and ideas, and the capacity to turn them into physical reality.

The poor man is the one that does not have ideas because ideas are the seeds that guarantee a future harvest.

Money flows in the direction of ideas. To prosper life, you must begin with prosperity consciousness. You must see yourself as a rich person from the inside. The quality of the ideas flowing through your mind determincs the quality of your life.

I challenge you today to **DREAM BIG with IDEAS and SUCCEED**

CHAPTER 9: UNDERSTANDING THE POWER OF PURPOSE

> *"Definiteness of purpose is the starting point of all achievement."*
> **W. Clement Stone**

Everything in life is controlled and governed by the power of purpose. Nothing exists on earth without a peculiar purpose. Just as no one embarks on any project without a specific reason for doing so, in the same way, God never went into production until He had concluded the purpose that His products would serve on earth. Everything in life exists for a specific purpose. Therefore, you are a product of purpose. And that is your dream.

When you do not know the purpose of a product, all you will do is to abuse it.

Dr. Myles Munroe once said; "When purpose is not known, abuse is inevitable."

To abuse something is to use it abnormally. As a matter of fact, the word 'abuse' came from a combination of two words; abnormal and use. So 'abuse' simply means; abnormal usage of a thing.
At the root of every form of frustration in life is lack of understanding of purpose. The glory of a man is in the fulfillment of God's purpose for his life.

That was why Dr. Martin Luther King Jnr. said; "If a man has no purpose for living, he is not fit to live."

In order words, if you do not have a dream, you are fit to live because we live in the dreamers world

Therefore **DREAM BIG and SUCCEED** today as you discover your purpose for living.

CHAPTER 10: UNLEASH YOUR POTENTIAL

> *"It is necessary that we make the right choices, find out what our talents and abilities are and have them properly trained and fitted to achieve the desired end"*
> **E.W. Kenyon**

You cannot separate your potential from the fulfillment of your dream, just as you cannot separate a man from a woman to have a baby.

What you need to fulfill your dream is already in you in form of potential. Your only task is to discover it and harness it to bring you into your land of fulfillment.

The ability is in you, but your understanding of its usage is the key to your fulfillment. There is no one who is not gifted by God one way or the other.

You have within you all the qualities and elements

that are necessary to make you a success. Your major task is the development of that gift that God has already given you.

The best way to discover your full potential is to continually try to reach higher, go further, see over, and grasp something greater than you now know. Nobody knows who you are except God who has blessed you with potential. The most important principle of life is that God is a God of potential and he created everything with potential.

Your success in life in the pursuit of your dream is not determined by the potential alone, but by what you do with that potential.

I challenge you today to **DISCOVER and UNLEASH your potential to achieve your DREAM.**

CHAPTER 11: YOU CAN ACHIEVE MORE THAN YOU HAVE

"Success in business requires training and discipline and hard work. But if you're not frightened by these things, the opportunities are just as great today as they ever were."
David Rockefeller

Success is the continuous journey towards the achievement of predetermined worthwhile goals. There is always a place called "FORWARD". In life we can never get to a place where we think we have arrived because we have the opportunity to achieve more than we have ever achieved.

I believe that the greatest enemy of progress is our last success and the greatest enemy of success is success itself. We should not allow our last success to stop us from pushing for bigger and higher levels of success. Catherine Ponder said; "Why settle for so little in life when you can have so much just by daring to be different in your thinking."

In his Arizona State Commencement Speech of the year 2009, Barack Obama, the first African-American President of the United States of America said; "I've come to embrace the notion that I haven't done enough in my life. I've come to confirm that one's title, even a title like president of the United States, says very little about how well one's life has been led. No matter how much you've done or how successful you've been, there's always more to do, always more to learn, and always more to achieve."

Friend, resolve today to keep **DREAMING BIG**, pushing for higher levels of success and you will grow bigger to impact your world.

CHAPTER 12: YOUR ATTITUDE DETERMINE YOUR ALTITUDE

Attitude is everything because it is involved in everything. It impacts our performance at work and our relationship. Attitude is the cornerstone upon which we build our lives.
Keith Harrell

There is nothing as powerful as attitude. All our responses to life's issues are dictated by our attitudes. In other words, it is attitude that determines our reactions to the present and decides the quality of our future. Attitude that is not controlled will control you because it is attitude that creates your world and designs your destiny.

The dictionary defines attitude as a manner, disposition, feeling, and position with regard to a person or thing; a tendency or orientation of the mind.

Attitude is the way you mentally look at the world around you. It is how you view your environment and your future. Attitude means mindset or mental conditioning that determines our interpretation of and our response to things happening within and around us. Attitude is the servant that can open the doors of life or close the gates of possibilities.

W. W. Ziege said; "Nothing can stop the man with the right mental attitude from achieving his goal; noting on earth can help the man with the wrong mental attitude."

Your attitude determines your altitude. How you perceive and interpret events in your life will determine how far in life you will go in your pursuit. Your success is really very much dependent on your attitude.

Therefore, **DREAM BIG** with the right **ATTITUDE and you will SUCCEED.**

CHAPTER 13 YOUR DREAM IS TO SERVE PEOPLE

The level of your greatness in life is a function of the level of your service to mankind.
Sunday A. Ezekiel

Service is the pathway to greatness in life. Until you are ready to serve, you are not prepared to shine. It takes stewardship to mount the throne of leadership.

Your dream is a seed from God and that seed was given to you for the purpose of improving the lot of other people. The fulfillment of your dream must bring happiness, joy, comfort and fulfillment to people.

Your dream in life should be a solution to the problems of the people around the world. Any dream that is self centered will end up as a doom.

During one of my recent studies on this subject of service, I come up with the following thoughts:

* Service is your ticket into the realm of glorification.
* If you refuse to serve others, you will be starved by others.
* Stardom is a direct product of service.
* Your shining in life is achieved by your service in life.
* To escape stinking is to embrace service.
* Sincere service ensures a secured future.
* The security of your destiny is a product of the sincerity of your service to mankind.
* The level of your greatness in life is a function of the level of your service to mankind.

You have no excuse for not getting involved in serving people. Service makes room for you to release your potential to the world.

I therefore challenge today to **DREAM BIG (by serving people) and SUCCEED**

CHAPTER 14: YOU CAN FAIL FORWARD TO ACHIEVE YOUR DREAM

Failure, like death and taxes, will happen. Your response to failure holds the key to your future.
John Maxwell

At some point, all great achievers are tempted to believe they are failures. But in spite of that, they persevere. In the face of adversity, shortcomings, and rejection, they hold onto self-belief and refuse to see themselves as failures.

Let us examine some principles for Failing Forward by John Maxwell

1. Reject Rejection: Achievers who persevere do not base their self-worth on their performance. On the contrary, they have a healthy self-image that's not dictated by external events. When they fall short, rather than labeling themselves a failure, they learn from mistakes in their judgment or behavior.

2. Don't Point Fingers: When people fail, they're often tempted to blame others for their lack of

success. By pointing fingers, they sink into a victim mentality and cede their fate to outsiders. When playing the blame game, people rob themselves of learning from their failures and alienate others by refusing to take responsibility for
mistakes.

3. See Failure as Temporary: People who personalize failure see a problem as a hole they're permanently stuck in, whereas achievers see any predicament as temporary. One mindset wallows in failure, the other looks forward to success. By putting mistakes into perspective, achievers are able to see failure as a momentary event, not a symptom of a lifelong epidemic.

4. Set Realistic Expectations: Unrealistic goals doom people to failure. For instance, if a person hasn't exercised for five years, then making it to a gym twice a week may be a better goal than running in next month's marathon. Also, some people insensibly expect to be perfect. Everyone fails, so expect setbacks and emotionally prepare to deal with them.

Your dream will not die with you. Use failure as your opportunity to create a glorious future for yourself. Therefore, **DREAM BIG and SUCCEED.**

CHAPTER 15
TURNING YOUR PAINS TO PROGRESS & YOUR SETBACKS TO SUCCESS

> *"It is interesting to notice how some minds seem almost to create themselves, springing up under every disadvantage, and working their solitary but irresistible way through a thousand obstacles.*
> ***Washington Irving***

Few years ago, I wrote these in one of by books:

"Great trials are often necessary to prepare us for great responsibilities

People who have never had difficulties or problems tend to be very shallow

No diamond or gem has ever been polished without friction

It is the irritation in the oyster that produces the pearl

Success consists of getting up just one more time than you fall

There is no mistake as great as the mistake of not going on

Men do not fail. They just give up easily

The greatest failure in life is to stop trying

There is no gain without pain

You will never reach some distant shore if you are afraid to leave the safety of the harbor

Even if you are on the right track, you will get run over if you just sit there

Commit yourself to something great and wonderful – something bigger than yourself

Adversities are divine opportunities for your advancement

You can advance in spite of adversities."

Yes, you can **DREAM BIG**, face your **ADVERSITY and SUCCEED.**

CHAPTER 16: AWAKEN THE BIG DREAM WITHIN YOU

> *"It's not what we do once in a while that counts, but our habitual actions. What ultimately determines who we become and where we go in life are our decisions. These decisions shape our destiny."*
> ***Anthony Robbins***

There are giants within every human, but until they are awaken they remain dwarfs.

It takes the process of dreaming big to awaken these giants. Every great events, business, career, organisation were sometimes dreams in the heart of the initiator or inventor. Your great business, career or organisation are the reality of the dream within you. You have a responsibility to bring the giant out of you to bless the world.

I like the way E.W. Kenyon describe the process of dreaming, he said, "Make your brain work. It will sweat; but make it work. It will improve. It will develop until you become a wonder to those around you."

There is a giant dream within you. It has the capacity of giving value to millions of people across the globe. You must awaken that giant. Destinies are waiting on you. You cannot afford to disappoint them.

Therefore, I challenge you today to **AWAKEN THE GIANT DREAM WITHIN YOU and SUCCEED.**

CHAPTER 17: BE INNOVATIVE IN YOUR THINKING

"Success in the 21st century flows directly from innovation, not optimization. It is not gained by perfecting the known, but by imperfectly seizing the unknown."
Kevin Kelly

Innovation simply means introduction of something new through creative thinking which are converted to marketable product or service.

It is the process of translating an idea or invention into a good or service that creates value or for which customers will pay. It is the application of better solutions that meet new requirements, unarticulated needs or existing market needs.

Your dream requires the engagement of your innovative mind to become a reality. And the more innovative your are in your thinking the better results you will achieve.

We live in a fast changing world and only those who change with the change can effectively achieve their dream. You cannot afford to keep thinking local and expect to achieve a global result. And global dreamers are innovative thinkers.

Therefore, **DREAM BIG, INNOVATE and SUCCEED**

CHAPTER 18: BUILD YOUR DREAM TEAM

> *"None of us is as smart as all of us".*
> ***Ken Blanchard***

Just as it is said that without vision the people perish, it is also true that without people dream will die.

No one can successfully carry out a dream without involving people. There is no way a single individual can fulfill a dream. If the dream is big enough, many people will be needed to carry out its object.

Effective leader working at the team level realize that to be good stewards of the energy and efforts of those committed to work with him, they must honour the power of diversity and acknowledge the power of teamwork.

It is your responsibility to locate the right people that will help you in carrying out the objects of your dream.

A team is a group of people coming together to collaborate. Team members are deeply committed to each other's personal growth and success. That commitment usually transcends the team.

As the team leader, you must carry everyone along in the task involve in the dream and it must be a mutually benefiting relationship. Everyone must be fully involved and know that your dream will improve their lives.

It is time to **DREAM BIG, build your DREAM TEAM and SUCCEED**

CHAPTER 19: CELEBRATE THE REALITY OF YOUR BIG DREAM

"If your dream dies, dream another one. If things don't work out the way you've planned, God has a better plan for you".
Joel Osteen

Greatness is a product of grace at work in a man. And grace is made available through continuous celebration. God demands that we recognize Him as the source and 'fulfiller' of our dreams in life. That is why we need to acknowledge Him at every stage of the pursuit of the dream He has given us.

Therefore, it is imperative that you develop the attitude of celebration of every level of result in your pursuit. It does not matter the kind or level of result – positive or negative, big or small- you need to celebrate it. It is a continuous celebration that guarantees a continuous flow of grace required to fulfill your dream. And celebration will turn negative results to positive ones.

Those who has developed the attitude of gratitude will continue to enjoy the hand of God in the fulfillment of their dreams.

As we end the month of May today, celebrate God for all He has done for you especially in the pursuit of your dream. The fact that you are still alive means there is a great hope of fulfillment of destiny.

I challenge you today to **CELEBRATE THE REALITY OF YOUR BIG DREAM**

CHAPTER 20: CHANGE YOUR THINKING, CHANGE YOUR LIFE

"Thought is the only power which can produce tangible riches from the Formless Substance. The stuff from which all things are made is a substance which thinks, and a thought of form in this substance produces the form."
Wallace D. Wattles

You are a direct product of your thoughts. It is the thoughts that dominate your mind that controls your life. Your life will move in the direction of your most dominant thoughts.

Your thought is the creator of your realities. If you do not like your present results, you have to change your present thought pattern. If I can access your thoughts, I can predict your future, because you are where you are by reason of your consistent thoughts and you will also find yourself in the future that your present thought is creating.

Mark Victor Hansen said; "Thoughts and ideas are the source of all wealth, success, material gain, all great discoveries, inventions and achievements"

The quality of your thoughts determine the quality of your life. Everything we see in the physical was first created in the realm of thoughts. To create a different result, you must think differently and challenge conventional thinking.

THE BEST WAY TO THINK
The best way to think is to think like God in whose image your are made.

Be a BIG THINKER. Big thinking precedes big achievement
Be a POSITIVE THINKER. Positive thinking produce positive result
Be a SUCCESS THINKER. Success thinking lead to success
Be a PEOPLE THINKER. Think of helping people and succeed
Be a FOCUSED THINKER. Focus your thought on what you want
Be a GREAT THINKER. Great thinking leads to great achievement
Be a PEACE THINKER. If you think peace, you will live in peace.

I therefore challenge you today to **CHANGE YOUR THINKING and SUCCEED**

CHAPTER 21: CREATING THE ACTUAL PICTURES OF YOUR DREAM

"Try to remember that the picture you think, feel and see is reflected into the Universal Mind, and by the natural law of reciprocal action must return to you in either spiritual or physical form."
Genevieve Behrend

Pictures are formed by your thought pattern and this eventually transforms into your dream in real life. There are pictures your have seen in a particular place many years ago that makes you remember what happened then. That is how powerful pictures can be.

When you begin to create the actual pictures of your dream and look at the pictures regularly, you will begin to move towards bringing those pictures into realities.

Bob Proctor, when describing the Law of Attraction said; "Everything coming into your life, you are attracting into your life. And it is attracted to you by virtue of the images (pictures) you are holding in your mind. Whatever is going on in your mind, you are attracting to you."

You need to have a VISION BOARD where you paste pictures of what you desire to have in your life. As you look at these pictures regularly, you are creating their reality step by step. The more you see it everyday, the more passionate you become in moving towards it. It is not enough to talk about it; it is very important that you paint it in pictures.

I admonish you today to **DREAM BIG** through **PICTURES and SUCCEED.**

CHAPTER 22: CREATIVE THINKING DIMENSION

> *"Thought is the only power which can produce tangible riches from the Formless Substance. The stuff from which all things are made is a substance which thinks, and a thought of form in this substance produces the form."*
> **Wallace D. Wattles**

Research has shown that only five percent of the human populations think. Fifteen percent think they are thinking and the remaining eighty percent will rather die than think.

The quality of the ideas flowing through your mind determines the quality of your life. Every word that a man pronounces is a product of an idea – his thoughts.

Creativity is the bringing into being of something which did not exist before, either as a product, a process or a thought.

Creative thinking is the process which we use when

we come up with a new idea. It is the merging of ideas which have not been merged before.

Real millionaires and billionaires are creative thinkers. They engage in a process of thinking that creates solutions to peoples problems.

To join the club of high achievers, you need to understand the power of creative thinking and engage it to help people solve their problems.

I hereby admonish you today to engage in creative thinking as you **DREAM BIG and SUCCEED**

CHAPTER 23 — DARE YOUR DREAM

'None of the Secret of Success will work unless you do; often, the simple answer to your problem is 'GO TO WORK'
John Mason

No man can fulfill any dream or vision without practical commitment to the tasks involved. However, for every dream to be fulfilled, the dreamer must dare the dream.

You are obligated to do the task involved in carrying out the dream. It is your decision to dare your dream that determines its ultimate accomplishment.
It takes practical commitment on the part of the dreamer to his dream to have the dream fulfilled.

According to George P. Burnham 'I can't do it' never yet accomplished anything; 'I will try' has performed wonders.

Life has its ways of testing every man, but if you are

determined you will always pass the tests of life and overcome every form of discouragement. Winning belongs to those who are resolutely determined, come what may. And there has never been a winner who did not first expect to win. Great people are ordinary people with extraordinary amount of determination.

The great leader Jim Rohn once noted, 'Do not let your learning lead to knowledge; let your learning lead to action.'

I therefore challenge you today to **DREAM BIG and SUCCEED.**

CHAPTER 24: DECIDE WHAT YOU WANT

'None of the Secret of Success will work unless you do; often, the simple answer to your problem is 'GO TO WORK'
John Mason

Rick Pitino once wrote, "Success will not happen unless you choose to make it happen. Success is not a lucky break. It is not a divine right. It is not an accident of birth. Success is a choice."

To achieve a millionaire dream, you have to decide exactly what you want and what to focus on. You have to decide on what you will spend your time on. You have to decide where you will go and where you will not go. Your decision has the power to push you into those things that are needed to be done in order to fulfill your dream.

It is a personal responsibility which you must accept

because, in any activity in life, the first step to success is decision making. And it is either you will decide for your life, or life will decide for you.

It was Robert Schuller who said, "The difference between the high achiever and low achiever is this: The high achiever almost always makes decisions before he's ready to move."

Join the club of the high achievers today as you **DREAM BIG and SUCCEED**

 DETERMINE TO WIN

> *"Be willing to be uncomfortable. Be comfortable being uncomfortable. It may get tough, but it's a small price to pay for living a dream."*
> **Peter Mcwilliams**

No one can fulfill a dream without paying the price of determination. Until you are resolutely determined, you cannot achieve the objects of your dream.

Determination is a major key for successful accomplishment. You have to be resolutely determined if you must turn your dream to reality. You must be doggedly determined to fulfill that dream or else you will tend to give up as a result of discouragement that will always come your way.

Winning belongs to those who are resolutely determined, come what may. And there has never been a winner who did not first determine to win. Great people are ordinary people with extraordinary amount of determination.

It was Abraham Lincoln who said, "Always bear in mind that your own resolution to succeed is more important than any other one thing."

When you determine that the thing can and shall be done, you will find the way, because the hardest rock will yield to those who drill with determination.

Walt Disney who founded the world famous DISNEY WORLD once said, "All dreams can come true…if we have the courage to pursue them."

Your dream will come true as you develop the determination to see it through. Therefore, **DREAM BIG and SUCCEED with DETERMINATION**

CHAPTER 26: DISCOVER YOUR PURPOSE

> *"I have brought myself, by long meditation, to the conviction that a human being with a settled purpose must accomplish it, and that nothing can resist a will which will stake even existence upon its fulfillment."*
> **Benjamin Disraeli**

Our decisions in life are the determinants of all that happen to us in life. If you decide to discover and pursue your life purpose, you will become exactly what you pursue. It is your decision that creates your future.

Basically, your purpose is the end goal that drives your current actions. It's the reason that you work on the things you do, the outcome you wish to achieve by your efforts.

Success in life is the fulfillment of the original intent or purpose established by the manufacturer of a product or the initiator and source of an assignment.

You cannot measure your success by comparing what you have done in life with what others have done; rather, your success is measured by comparing what you have done with what you are created to do.
Michel de Montaigne once said; "The soul which has no fixed purpose in life is lost; to be everywhere, is to be nowhere".

When you discover your purpose, you will never try to be like someone else. The best you can become is you. You are created an original; the only number one you. If you try to be like someone else, you end up as number two of that person and you lose you own identity.

Friend, I admonish you today to **DREAM BIG, DISCOVER YOUR PURPOSE and SUCCEED**

CHAPTER 27: DO YOU HAVE A MISSION STATEMENT?

"I would like to repeat the critical importance of committing your plan to writing. It cannot be overemphasized!"
Paul J. Meyer

Your ability to describe your dream with a single statement is very important to bringing that to reality. That is what I called a Mission Statement.

It is your Mission Statement that defines your pursuit. I cannot describe you without know your Mission Statement.

I defined a Mission Statement as one statement that describes what you want to accomplish in life. It is just one statement, though it could be a combination of sentences in form of compound or complex sentence, but it is just a statement describing what you stand for in life.

Susan Ward, a Management Expert, defines Mission Statement as a brief description of a company's fundamental purpose both for those in the organization and for the public.

Your Mission Statement must be in line with your dream. I know that your dream has the possibility of becoming a reality, but you need to reduce the details of that dream into one statement called a "Mission Statement".

For instance, my own Mission Statement based on my dream is *To Equip, Empower and Establish People for Impact & Exploits through a discovery of their dream, vision and purpose in life.*

Everything I am doing is pointing towards the realization of that Mission Statement which came out of my dream.

What is your dream in life? Use that dream to develop a Mission Statement that will give shape and meaning to your life as you read the statement to yourself. This is the key to fulfilling your dream in life

DREAM BIG and SUCCEED.

CHAPTER 28: DREAMERS ARE COMMITTED LEARNERS

> *Towards Mental Exploits "No matter how gifted you are, how studious you are is what determines how colourful you will become mentally."*
> **David Oyedepo**

Dreamers make sacrifices to seek knowledge. They read books; attend seminars, specialized training and workshops all in an attempt to learn what they need to know in order to succeed in leadership.

The highest possession of a leader is his personal collection of books. He is a consummate reader who is always looking for opportunities to improve his knowledge base through a never-ending process of learning. He creates his our learning opportunities which facilitate his educational environment.

Self-cultivation is a passion for personal development. True leaders possess a desire and commitment to gain knowledge and insight and to keep improving themselves by learning from others.

John F. Kennedy once said; "Leadership and learning are inseparable to each other."

If you desire to fulfill your dream and maximize your opportunities for leadership, you need to pay attention to your daily opportunities to grow by commitment to continuous learning.

Therefore, **DREAM BIG, LEARN NEW THINGS DAILY and SUCCEED**

CHAPTER 29: DREAMERS ARE LEADERS WITH A DARING SPIRIT

> *"Leadership: The capacity and will to rally people to a common purpose together with the character that inspires confidence and trust"*
> ***Field Marshal Montgomery***

Your dream makes you a leader who is curious and daring. Until you are ready to venture daringly, you cannot lead successfully. Leaders are those who are willing to dare the impossible in order to achieve the incredible.

A leader is a pacesetter, trail blazer and risk taker. He is willing to take calculated risk, step out in faith and try new things by challenging convention. A leader is not afraid of failure and mistake because, he knows that every adversity sows a seed of equivalent success. He believes that the difference between greatness and mediocrity is often how an individual views a mistake.

A true leader goes to where others are not willing to go and creates a path for those who are coming. He is very brave and courageous. A leader is willing to take risks today for something better tomorrow.

The great leadership coach, John C. Maxwell once said; "A man must be big enough to admit his mistakes, smart enough to profit from them, and strong enough to correct them."

Also, a leader understands that hard things are put in our way, not to stop us, but to call out our courage and strength. He operates with the knowledge of the fact that we gain strength, courage and confidence by every experience in which we really stop to look fear in the face and do the thing we think we cannot do.

Become a leader as you **DREAM BIG and SUCCEED**

CHAPTER 30: EXPECTATION: YOUR WINNING KEY

"High expectation is the key to everything."
Sam Walton

Your expectation has power to determine what comes your way in life. If you are going to fulfill your dream, you must expect to win. Your fire of expectation must be burning high. Expectation is what gives birth to manifestation. No matter how big your dream is, how high your expectation to win is what will ultimately determine how successful you become in the race of life. Your attitude to life is the product of your expectation.

John C. Maxwell the great leadership guru said; "When you change your expectation you change your attitude; when you change your attitude, you change your behaviour; when you change your behaviour, you change your performance."

That statement simply shows that your performance in life is dictated by your expectation in life. Expectation of success will lead to success while expectation of failure will lead to failure.

I believe that the first and most important step toward success is the expectation that we can succeed in what we do. The reason is because you will see exactly what you expect to see in your life.

The great hero, Benjamin Franklin put it this way; "Blessed is the one who expects nothing, for he shall receive it."

Expectation is your hope of what will happen in your future. If what you hope to see negates what you dream to achieve, you may never achieve that dream, because what you expect does not correlate with what you dream.

I challenge you today to **DREAM BIG, EXPECT TO WIN and SUCCEED**

CHAPTER 31: FOCUS ON YOUR DREAM

> *"Nothing stops the man who desires to achieve. Every obstacle is simply a course to develop his achievement muscle. It's a strengthening of his powers of accomplishment."*
> **Eric Butterworth**

There is power in a focused attention. It is the ability to direct the attention to one single thought or subject, to the exclusion of everything else. The more clearly focused we are on exactly what we want, the easier and faster we will manifest everything we need to make it a physical reality.

Successful people understand that focus is a key ingredient to the success of their business. They know the importance of identifying and concentrating on making the unique aspects of their business and careers as superb as possible. They are clear on what their business stands for, and stick to it.

Also, to become a success, you need to keep your eyes on the prize and spend your resources, time and energy in focusing on the attainment of your goals, which include running and developing a successful, profitable and viable business through your vision or dream.

It has been scientifically proven that a magnifying glass could burn a piece of paper when the rays of the sun were focused through it. The fire could start only when the sun's rays were concentrated to a small point. When the magnifying glass was moved too far away or too close to the paper, the rays were not focused enough and nothing happened. That simply explains the place of being focused in a bid to accomplish success in life. Focus is an attitude that cannot be overemphasized if success is to be accomplished.

Therefore, **DREAM BIG, FOCUS ON YOUR BIG DREAM and SUCCEED**

CHAPTER 32: GREAT ACHIEVERS ARE GOALS ORIENTED

"In life, as in football, you won't go far unless you know where the goal posts are."
Arnold Glasow

A goal is a dream with a date on it, because, a goal is nothing more than a dream with a time limit.

A goal can be defined as the end result of ultimate accomplishment toward which an effort is directed. A goal is the mark desired to hit; the sign post to ones end; a state of affairs that a man intended to achieve and which terminates when achieved

Elements of Goals

Uniqueness: - Your goal must be unique because your dream is not the same as other people's dreams and you are the one who set your goal.

Inspirational: - Inspiration means to be inspired. Your goal is based on your inspired thought that is;

the dream of your heart. That goal must inspire you to move towards your dream.

Specificity: - Goals are specific things you want to accomplish. It must not be a vague mind description of your desire, but a specific object of your desire.

Documentation: - Your goal must be clearly written down so that you will always know what to do.

Realizable: - Your goal must be a realizable one. You know what you can achieve, so be realistic based on the facts available to you.

Harmonimity: - Your goal should be in harmony with your core values & beliefs. It must align with your dream.

Time bound: - Your goal must be with date. There must be a time limit on your goal. That means there is a time to begin and a time to end.

Arise and **DREAM BIG with specific goals and you will SUCCEED**

CHAPTER 33: IF YOU CAN SEE IT, YOU CAN GET IT

*"If you can imagine it, you can achieve it.
If you can dream it, you can become it".*
William Arthur Ward

Dreams are powerful in creating a future for man. That is why everyone who desires a great future needs to have a very good understanding of the subject of dream.

It is a well known truth that every empire in the world today is built by a dream in the heart of man. Also, there are still great empires that will be built in this world as products of the great dreams in the hearts of certain men who do not look like great men now.

I believe that the twenty-first century's great accomplishment will outweigh those of earlier centuries; but the truth is that twenty-first century men must learn how to dream greater dreams and follow after their dreams.

Success in every endeavour of man is traceable to the dream of man. No man can fulfill a divine mandate without engaging the power of dream. In other words, the reason for failure in the race of life is a direct product of lack of dream. One person with a dream can accomplish more than one hundred others without one.

It was Zig Ziglar who said, "If you can dream it, then you can achieve it."

If you really desire to move from where you are now to a better place, your ability to **DREAM BIG is the key. Therefore, DREAM BIG and SUCCEED**

CHAPTER 34: IMPROVE YOURSELF TO FULFIL YOUR DREAM

> *"Anyone who stops learning is old, whether at twenty or eighty. Anyone who keeps learning stays young. The greatest thing in life is to keep your mind young."*
> **Henry Ford**

Self improvement through constant learning has the capacity to unlock the great potential for successful achievement and speedy fulfillment of your dream.

Learning is a must if you must grow. The day you stopped learning is the day you stopped growing and you must keep growing if you must advance against all adversities to fulfill your dream.

Dr. David Oyedepo once said; "No matter how gifted you are, it is how studious you are that determines how colourful you will become mentally".

Learning is an activity of the mind because the mind

has the ability to acquire and store information which can be utilized for making decisions in order to advance in life.

That is why it is important to not stop learning, because, the day a man stops learning is the day he starts dying, no matter how old or young. That is the reality of life.

No one has ever become a success in life without having taken the time to learn all about his pursuits. The truth is the more learned you are in your field, the more command you gain and ultimately, the more respect you earn. This is because at the point of knowledge, you make tremendous advancement against all adversities of life and emerge a hero in your field of endeavour.

Your dream in life is your area of assignment and you need to keep improving yourself daily in that aspect so as to get to your desired end.

I challenge you today to **DREAM BIG, IMPROVE YOURSELF** daily through constant learning and you will **SUCCEED.**

CHAPTER 35: MASTER YOUR MIND TO ACHIEVE YOUR DREAM

"The mind is the master weaver, both of the inner garment of character and the outer garment of circumstance."
James Allen

Stop and think of how the past affects you. There are probably episodes in your personal history that have shaped your life. It is your beliefs that dictate your life experience. If you can or can't do something it often depends whether you think you can or can't. In other words, mastering mind power has a lot to do with mastering your beliefs.

Your beliefs about what is possible for you come from experience. You didn't emerge from the womb with a belief about your ability. You didn't arrive on your birth day believing that your income would be minimal, your health poor, or that you would choose the wrong mate. These types of ideas are learned through experience.

They could have come from your perception of something you personally experienced that led you to believe that you weren't capable or deserving enough. Or those ideas could have come from an experience that you had of ANOTHER person's perceptions -- like in the case of a parent telling a child something they believe to be true.

You have enormous freedom to change your memories, even create new memories, and let those new memories serve as a basis for beliefs that make success more likely and possible.

You can create beliefs that help you in the process of mastering your mind power and adopting a millionaire mindset. You can change memories (and therefore beliefs) with self hypnosis and other mind power techniques with the use of visualization.

Your ability to change your memories helps you change your beliefs to those one that can help you achieve your dream.

I challenge you today to **DREAM BIG, MASTER YOUR MIND and SUCCEED.**

CHAPTER 36: NEVER GIVE UP ON YOUR DREAM

> *"The strongest oak of the forest is not the one that is protected from the storm and hidden from the sun. It's the one that stands in the open where it is compelled to struggle for its existence against the winds and rains and the scorching sun. Effort only fully releases its reward after a person refuses to quit."*
> **Napoleon Hill**

There is nothing as powerful as a dream in the pursuit of a great future. Great men are men with great dreams who refused to give up on their dreams until they have accomplished its objects.

The dream you do not pursue or the one you quit or give up on, you cannot fulfill.

Those who have won in the race of life are those who refused to quit in spite of all odds. Also, those who have failed are those who quit and gave up the pursuit of their dreams as a result of fear, procrastination and/or impatience. If you will hold on just one more time, you will discover that you are very close to your dreamland of fulfillment. It may be that the next appointment you have is what will bring you closer to the fulfillment of your long awaited dream, though several previous ones failed. Those ones that failed in the past are just part of the process that you will have to go through to get you to the one that will be successful.

I admonish you today to **DREAM BIG, NEVER GIVE UP and you will SUCCEED.**

CHAPTER 37: PAY THE PRICE FOR YOUR DREAM

Nothing of value comes cheap. Your dream will not deliver on its own. You must pay the price to achieve it.
Sunday A. Ezekiel

Your readiness to go the extra mile in paying the price is what determines your outcome in life. Only those who pay the PRICE can win the PRIZE.

God has placed your destiny in your hand and it is your responsibility to fulfill it.
Until your accept 100% responsibility for your life, you will live like a liability in the world

No one ever become great in life without paying the required price for greatness and according Winston Churchill, RESPONSIBILITY IS THE PRICE FOR GREATNESS.

Until you stop giving excuses, you can never experience a lasting success

You will never leave where you are until you decide where you would rather be.

Therefore, arise today to **PAY THE PRICE FOR YOUR DREAM**

CHAPTER 38: PLAN TO FULFIL YOUR DREAM

> *"Success does not require a super intellect. It does require a dream with PLANS to reach a goal".*
> **Ken Gaub**

Planning is a major key to accomplishment of any given task in life. Only those who develop a plan can fulfill the objects of their dream. A plan is the road-map to your destination. Your destination is the fulfillment of your dream, but the map to get you there is the plan you have to develop.

Also, a plan is the architectural design for the house you are to build. Your dream is likened to a building, but there has to be a clear design in place to follow in putting up the building. Your dream is your destiny placed in front of your, but your plan is the step by step road-map that you will follow to take you to that destiny

Lester R. Bittel, the author of The Nine Master Keys of Management said; "Good plans shape good decisions. That's why good planning helps to make elusive dreams come true."

No one has ever built a house without a building plan. No successful business or empire is ever built in life without a blueprint. The blueprint is the plan. In your plan, the details of how you will relate with people, how you will acquire the relevant skills, how you will acquire the material and financial resources and how you are going to utilize and coordinate them for the fulfillment of your dream must be put into consideration.

Friend, it is time begin to **DREAM BIG and SUCCEED by wise planning.**

CHAPTER 39: PRESS ON WITH FOCUS

> *"When every physical and mental resource is focused, one's power to solve a problem multiplies tremendously."*
> **Norman Vincent Peale**

Winning in the race of life is not for those who begin; rather, it is for those who finished the race. It is not just starting that matters; finishing what you have started is what determines how you will end. Only those who finished will win the prize, but it takes paying the price to win the prize. One of the prices to pay is the price of focus.

Focus is a powerful force that adds speed to the accomplishment of your dream and arrival at your glorious destiny. Being focus on your dream has tremendous power to bring it to reality.

Focus simply means, main emphasis: concentrated effort or attention on a particular thing.

There is power in a focused attention. It is the ability to direct the attention to one single thought or subject, to the exclusion of everything else for accomplishing one's dream The more clearly focused we are on exactly what we want, the easier and faster we will manifest everything we need to make it a physical reality.

When our mind is focused, our energies are not dissipated on irrelevant activities or thoughts. Disciplined focus is what distinguished those who make things happen from those who watch things happen.

Successful people understand that focus is a key ingredient to the success of their business. They know the importance of identifying and concentrating on making the unique aspects of their business and careers as superb as possible. They are clear on what their business stands for, and stick to it.

I challenge you today to **DREAM BIG. PRESS ON and BE FOCUSED. You will SUCCEED.**

CHAPTER 40: PROBLEMS ARE YOUR OPPORTUNITIES FOR PROGRESS

"Every adversity holds within it the seed of undeveloped possibilities"
Robert Schuller

Your perception of issue are very important in determining how you will achieve your dream. And it is not what actually happens to you that really matter but how you perceive and respond that matter.

How you you see problems? In what ways do you respond to them? Do you accept responsibility to solve problems or you shy away from them?

Sometimes our real blessings often appear to us in the shape of pains, losses and disappointments.

Your productivity is a product of your ability to take advantage of your adversities to bring you into a positive change from one level to another. The calamity or confusion you may have is not designed to leave you in the same position it met you, rather, it is orchestrated to produce the best out of you, and most time God is the force behind it. This is because He wants you to move on to the next level and you will have to pay the price.

Dale Carnegie once noted; "Develop success from failures. Discouragement and failure are two of the surest stepping stones to success."

It is the surmounting of difficulties that make heroes and he that can heroically endure adversity will bear prosperity with equal greatness of soul; for the mind that cannot be dejected by the former is not likely to be transported with the later. Many have had their greatness made for them by their enemies.

Understand that it is a rough road that leads to the heights of greatness and the difficulties you meet will resolve themselves as you advance. Proceed, and light will dawn, and shine with increasing clearness on your path.

Therefore, **DREAM BIG and SUCCEED as you solve PROBLEMS**

 PURSUE YOUR DREAM

"You will not do incredible things without an incredible dream."
John Eliot

You have the ability to attain whatever you seek; within you is every potential you can imagine. Always aim higher than you believe you can reach. So often, you'll discover that when your talents are set free by your imagination, you can achieve any goal.

If people offer their help or wisdom as you go through life, accept it gratefully. You can learn much from those who have gone before you. But never be afraid or hesitant to step off the accepted path and head off in your own direction if your heart tells you that it's the right way for you.

Always believe that you will ultimately succeed at whatever you do, and never forget the value of persistence, discipline, and determination. You are meant to be whatever you dream of becoming.

Dreams are extremely important, because, you cannot do anything successfully unless you can imagine it first.

One person with a dream can accomplish more than one hundred others without one. If you have a burning desire, you can accomplish anything. The biographies of great men and women are full of stories of how they did seemingly impossible things because they each had dream.

Dreaming is an act of pure imagination, attesting in all people a creative power, which if it were available in waking would make every man a great success.

However, no matter how great your dream is, you cannot achieve it unless you pursue it. It is the dream your go after that becomes a reality. This is because nothing works without someone working it out.
No one will work your dream for you because it is your dream not theirs. The man who desires success must have a dream of success and pursue that dream. Success comes through the pursuit of your dream.

Determine to **DREAM BIG, PURSUE YOUR BIG DREAM and SUCCEED**

CHAPTER 42: PURSUE YOUR DREAM WITH PASSION

> *"Enthusiasm is one of the most powerful engines of success. When you do a thing, do it with all your might. Put your whole soul into it. Stamp it with your own personality. Be active, be energetic and faithful, and you will accomplish your object. Nothing great was ever achieved without enthusiasm"*
> **Ralph Waldo Emerson**

It is not just having a big dream that result in success, rather, your attitude towards the pursuit of that big dream. Nothing great in the world has been accomplished without passion.

Passion is an attitude that must be present in the success equation. Doing something is not the key to success, it is how you are doing it that determines whether it will be successfully accomplished or not.

If there is no passion in your life, then have you really lived? Find your passion, whatever it may be.

Become it, and let it become you and you will find great things happen FOR you, TO you and BECAUSE of you.

Your dream has a great possibility of becoming a reality, but your passionate pursuit is a major requirement for it fulfillment.

I love the way Richard Branson puts it, "Ideally, since 80 percent of your life is spent working, you should start your business around something that is a passion of yours".

I admonish you today to **PURSUE YOUR BIG DREAM with PASSION.**

CHAPTER 43: P.U.S.H FOR YOUR DREAM

"Most men die from the neck up by the age of 25, because they stopped dreaming"
Benjamin Franklin

Success is cheap only if you know what to do and get to work doing it.

Your dream is the key to your desired success. And success in life is available to the individual who determined to succeed.

To fulfill your dream, you must learn how to P.U.S.H.

P stands for PERSIST. If you are known for giving up too easily, you cannot achieve your dream. You have a staying power or holding power to keep you going again and again until you get there.

U stands for UNLEASH. There is a power in you

which you must unleash to achieve your dream in life. You must unleash the power within to make you the person you have always wanted to be.

S stands for STRIVE. There has to be some level of striving towards something big before you can achieve it. You must keep trying, working and putting in your best until you get there.

H stands for HUSTLE. No one can achieve success without being ready to hustle. Get to work everyday until you get to where you want to be.

I therefore challenge you today to **P.U.S.H as you DREAM BIG and SUCCEED.**

CHAPTER 44 — REFUSE TO QUIT ON YOUR DREAM

"In the end, you're measured not by how much you undertake but by what you finally accomplish".
Donald Trump

Those who have won in life are those who refuse to quit in the pursuit of their dreams. If success is your desire, quitting is not a thing to consider. Life will always present to you opportunity to stop pursuing your dream through its waves of adversities, but what must be important to you is the end result which is the reality of your dream.

You are very close to your fulfillment than when you begin. That is why you cannot consider looking back at this very crucial stage.

Dr Michael Smurfit said; "Never accept failure, no matter how often it visits you. Keep going. Never give up. Never."

It is always too early to quit trying. If you seems to have fallen down now, rise up again and keep going. You cannot succeed by quitting because it's uncomfortable.

Success achievement is not always comfortable. It is that discomfort that makes great heroes. You must embrace it as part of the process of reaching your dreamland.

Thomas Edison said; "Many of life's failures are people who did not realize how close they were to success when they gave up."

I believe you very close to the end which will bring you out into the lime light. Therefore, **DREAM BIG. NEVER GIVE UP. AND YOU WILL SUCCEED.**

CHAPTER 45 RELEASING YOUR POTENTIAL

> *"Without ambition one starts nothing, and without hard work one finishes nothing. Therefore, those who stretch their backbone to reach their wish bone will make things happen."*
> ***Janice Krouskop***

It is only in the dictionary that you will see that success comes before work. But in real life, it is work before success. Work must come first before success can be achieved. Successful accomplishment of a dream is a direct product of hard work.

Work is God's way of revealing your talents, abilities and capabilities. When you have a dream, then it is time to work out its fulfillment and that requires the use of your potential, but that potential is released by hard work. Work arises from the desire to contribute to the world's wealth and well-being by giving of what you have been given by God in form of potential.

It is only through work that you can do and become all that God originally intended for your life. God does not give potential for fun; He expects it to be released as you work it out through committed, smart and creative work. Potential without work remains untapped. It remains unused and untested. Another way to define work is the use of your God given abilities and faculties to do or perform a task.

It takes work to achieve greatness. No one talks about greatness without work. Work is not the same as a job. It is not a job that releases potential, it is work. Job only provides you a pay cheque at the end of the month.
Job means; 'Just Over Broke' that is, one pay cheque away from being evicted.

I challenge you today to **DREAM BIG, RELEASE YOUR POTENTIAL and SUCCEED.**

CHAPTER 46: SET GOALS FOR YOUR DREAM

> *"Direction is simply the exercise of planning how you are going to get from Point A to Point B and then focusing on it."*
> **Donald Goss**

A goal can be defined as the end result of ultimate accomplishment toward which an effort is directed. A goal is the mark desired to hit; the sign post to ones end; a state of affairs that a man intended to achieve and which terminates when achieved.

A goal is a dream with a date on it, because, a goal is nothing more than a dream with a time limit.

Arnold Glasow once said; "In life, as in football, you won't go far unless you know where the goal posts are."

Goal setting is very essential to the fulfillment of your dream and you must commit to it.

To set goals means to define a course of action without distraction; to burn the bridge; to bring oneself under an oath; to declare one's fixed and unalterable decision.

David J. Schwarz in his book "The Magic of Thinking Big" wrote; "Nothing happens; no forward steps are taken until a goal is established."

Your goal must be SMART compliant, i.e. Specific, Measurable, Achievable, Realistic and Time bound.

I challenge you today to **SET GOAL for your BIG DREAM and SUCCEED.**

CHAPTER 47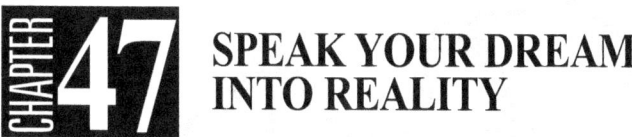
SPEAK YOUR DREAM INTO REALITY

> *"A man with a scant vocabulary will almost certainly be a weak thinker. The richer and more copious one's vocabulary and the greater one's awareness of fine distinctions and subtle nuances of meaning, the more fertile and precise is likely to be one's thinking. Knowledge of things and knowledge of the words for them grow together. If you do not know the words, you can hardly know the thing."*
> **Henry Hazlitt**

The spoken word has a tremendous impact on both your external and internal reality. Whatever you say eventually comes back to you like a boomerang.

Your mouth set the course of your result in life. Success or failure, it is all about what you say and keep saying.

Words filled with faith are the most powerful force in

the entire world. If God's Words created His world and you are dealt with a measure of His kind of faith, your own words will create your world. Your words dominate you. Your words put you over or under, depending on the content of it – positive or negative.
Our faith will never rise above the words that we keep speaking from our lips. It is faith confessions that create realities.

I dare you to develop a robust vocabulary based on the dream you intent to accomplish. And as you keep saying those words everyday, you are creating the reality. It is not what you say once that determines what you get, rather, it is what you say over and over again with faith that determines your outcome in life.

Begin to call yourself what you see yourself becoming based on your dream.
DREAM BIG, SPEAK BOLDLY and SUCCEED.

CHAPTER 48: STAND OUT & FULFILL YOUR DREAM

> "The majority of people meet with failure because they lack the persistence to create new plans to take the place of failed plans."
> **Mark Victor Hansen**

It is very important to note that God has placed your destiny in your hand and it is your responsibility to fulfill it. And until your accept 100% responsibility for your life, you will live like a liability in the world.

No one ever become great in life without paying the required price for greatness and according Winston Churchill, RESPONSIBILITY IS THE PRICE FOR GREATNESS. Until you stop giving excuses, you can never experience a lasting success and you cannot shine forth in life without arising from darkness in the world. Also, you will never leave where you are until you decide where you would rather be.

Ken Gaub said, "Success does not require a super

intellect. It does require a dream with PLANS to reach a goal."

Your ability to dream big and follow your dream is what will make you to stand out in the world. IT IS YOUR DREAM THAT CREATES YOUR FUTURE. The dreams of yesterday are the realities of today and the dreams of today will be the realities of tomorrow. It is dream that creates the future you and I are expecting. That means, if you don't have any dream today, there is no future to expect.

All the dreamers I know are international figures who are well known for their great accomplishments. It was their dreams of yesterday that brought them into global recognition today. Dream has the capacity of making you a global celebrity.

I challenge you today to **STAND OUT with your BIG BREAM and you will SUCCEED.**

CHAPTER 49: STOP PROCRASTINATING: ACT NOW!

"A common quality of successful, happy people is that they are action oriented. When they hear a good idea, they take action on it immediately to see if it can help them."
Brian Tracy

There is no way any one who indulges continuously in the act of procrastination can fulfill a dream.

The truth is that, the more you procrastinate on the tasks involved in your dream, the farther away you are from the fulfillment of that dream. That is why it is not every dream that gets to the stage of fulfillment, many have died prematurely.

If you are going to fulfill you dream, you must get rid of that attitude of procrastination, because, the dream you do not act upon, the object you cannot accomplish.

Don Marquis once said; "Procrastination is the art of

keeping up with yesterday."

When you possess the attitude of prompt action, it can affect every phase of your life. It can help you do the things you should do but do not feel like doing. Also, it can keep you from procrastinating when an unpleasant duty faces you, but it can also help you do those things that you want to do. It will help you seize those precious moments that, if lost, may never be retrieved.

It is time to get up, **DREAM BIG, ACT ON YOUR DREAM and SUCCEED**

CHAPTER 50: STUMBLING BLOCKS ARE YOUR STEPPING STONES

> *"All men dream but not equally. Those who dream by night in the dusty recesses of their minds wake in the day to find that it was vanity; but the dreamers of the day are dangerous men, for they may act their dream with open eyes to make it possible."*
> **T.E. Lawrence**

I believe that any adversity that does not destroy you will makes you stronger. Once you have faced those stumbling blocks and stared them down, you have the ability to calmly deal with other barriers while those who have never faced adversity question their own ability.

And looking throughout the pages of history at those who have accomplished the feats that we all aspire to, you will find that the seeds of their greatness were planted in their own stumbling blocks. Their seeds were fertilized with failure and watered with the blood, sweat, and tears of personal struggle.

The next time you face adversity, disappointment, or discouragement, realize that in that situation lies the seed of a greater tomorrow.

You can learn how to turn the stumbling blocks that stand in your way to stepping stone that will lead you to your dreamland of great achievement.

Nothing is predestined: The obstacles of your past can become the gateways that lead to new beginnings. It has been my philosophy of life that difficulties vanish when faced boldly.

It is important to note that good fortune and bad are equally necessary to man, to fit him to meet the contingencies of this life.

Charles Caleb Colton once noted, "Times of great calamity and confusion have ever been productive of the greatest minds. The purest ore is produced from the hottest furnace, and the brightest thunderbolt is elicited from the darkest storm."

It is imperative to know that adversity is like yeast. When the heat is turned up, it rises and the hotter it gets, the more it rises. Every opportunity that God brings our ways will always attract obstacles but we have the responsibility of rising above them.

Therefore, **DREAM BIG and SUCCEED as you turn your stumbling blocks to stepping stones.**

CHAPTER 51
SUCCESS IS IN YOU; BRING IT OUT!

> *"It is necessary that we make the right choices, find out what our talents and abilities are and have them properly trained and fitted to achieve the desired end"*
> **E.W. Kenyon**

Your are created to succeed, not to fail. Your success is in you in potential form, but you have a responsibility to bring it out.

We all possess the ability to reach the top of our own unique 'Mount Everest'. True success is not so much about being talented as it is about what you do with that talent. Even though God has given you potential in form of talent; the purpose of those gifts is to fulfill your God-given dream in life.

Potential is the sum total of who you are that you are yet to reveal. Your potential is what God deposited in you that can change your world.

The best way to discover your full potential is to

continually try to reach higher, go further, see over, and grasp something greater than you now know. The most important principle of life is that God is a God of potential and he created everything with potential.

To fulfill your dream, you must discover, develop, release and maximize your potential.

The power is in you, therefore, I challenge you to bring it out to achieve your dream.

CHAPTER 52: THE POWER OF ASSOCIATION

"You must constantly ask yourself these questions: Who am I around? What are they doing to me? What have they got me reading? What have they got me saying? Where do they have me going? What do they have me thinking? And most important, what do they have me becoming? Then ask yourself the big question: Is that okay? Your life does not get better by chance, it gets better by change."
Jim Rohn

The people around you determine what you are becoming. If you hang around negative people, you become a negative person. If they are positive, you become a better and positive person.

Your friends have a lot to do in your life; that is why you must make a wise choice for good and purpose-driven friendship. When you use iron to strike another iron, you will discover that the sparks that fly from that contact are very stimulating, especially when it is done in a dark place. That is how stimulating and refreshing it is when there is mutual and purpose-driven networking between two friends.

Dr. Stephen Covey who said; "One of the best ways to educate our hearts is to look at our interaction with other people, because our relationships with others are fundamentally a reflection of our relationship with ourselves."

To achieve the objects of your dream, you must carefully select your company. Even if you have business partners who are negative, do not allow their negativity contaminate your optimism.

Your dream has a great possibility, you cannot afford to play down of the importance of association in the pursuit of your dream.

Who are you keeping company with? They are have a lot to do in determining your future. Therefore, be wise in the choice of your relationships.

DREAM BIG today and SUCCEED.

CHAPTER 53: THE VIRTUE OF PATIENCE

> *"If I have ever made any valuable discoveries, it has been owing more to patient attention, than to any other talent."*
> **Isaac Newton**

The virtue of patience is a fundamental requirement in the fulfillment of your dream. Until patience is in place, you are not a candidate for a fulfilled destiny. Every one who has ever accomplished any great thing in the world has been known to possess this great virtue of patience.

To keep doing the same thing over and over again in an attempt to solve a particular problem, patience is required. Without patience, you cannot be diligent in your pursuit and without diligence, fulfillment is not in view. Patience is of utmost important in the race of life. It takes patience to persist and persevere in the pursuit of your dream until the end result is achieved. John Quincy Adams once said; "Patience and perseverance have a magical effect before which difficulties disappear and obstacles vanish."

Donald Trump once said that he worked on a project for about seventeen years trying to get approval from the required authority before he could start the project. Then he asked, "How many people can be patient for seventeen years working on a project before its take off?" He concluded with this statement, "That is why we don't have many billionaires."

There is power in continuity. It takes a continuous effort to get to the finishing line. There are many things in life that requires a daily commitment in order to accomplish a great result, but it takes grace of continuity to remain committed to such things. And that grace for continuity is a product of the virtue of patience at work in us.

The zeal needed to continue until the end result is accomplished comes with patience. Only those who continued patiently to the end can obtain the end result.

Therefore, be challenged today to **DREAM BIG and be patient. You will SUCCEED.**

GET CONNECTED

In case you have read this book and you are yet to receive Jesus as your personal Lord and Savior, please, say these words as your act of submission to God's redemption plan:

Thank you Heavenly Father for sending Your Son Jesus to save me. Lord Jesus, I believe that you died and resurrected to save me, I ask that you come into my life today. Forgive me of my sin, cleanse me with your blood and accept me in the beloved. I confess you as my Lord and Savior today. Now I know that I am born again and saved from sin and the world. Thank you Lord for saving me. Amen.

I congratulate you for making this great decision today and I pray that you will not fall apart in your walk with God in this new-found faith in Christ.

If this book has been of great blessing to you, please write us through our emails or send SMS or give us a call through our phones numbers to share your testimonies. You can also connect with us through our Facebook pages and website.

Do not fail to recommend this book to other people as a way of being a blessing to them in contributing to the fulfillment of their God-ordained purposes in life.

In addition, we welcome your comments and views about the book so as to know how we can serve you and other people in a better way.

Thank you. We love you

Pastor Sunday A. Ezekiel being commissioned to the ministry by his spiritual father, Bishop David O. Oyedepo on the 20th of April 2012

Pastor Sunday A. Ezekiel with Rev. Sam Adeyemi, 2015 and 2017

OTHER BOOKS BY THE SAME AUTHOR

1. Become The Best! Release Your Potential
2. Dream Big and Succeed
3. Living Your Vision
4. Purpose Power Secrets
5. Your Dream Creates Your Future

ABOUT THE AUTHOR

Sunday Adeniyi Ezekiel is an ordained Pastor, Insightful Teacher, Creative and Innovative Leadership Coach, with a visionary mandate to raise a people of impact and Exploits.

Ordained into an independent ministry by Bishop David Oyedepo of Living Faith Church a.k.a. Winners Chapel International after serving as a Pastor for some years in the headquarters in Canaan Land.

He is the President and Senior Pastor of DREAMERS WORLD CHRISTIAN CENTRE (a.k.a Faith Impact Chapel Int'l) Lagos, Nigeria. As an astute business magnate with a passion to help people create lasting wealth, he is the co-founder, Executive Director and member of the

Board of Directors of RICHLIFE COMMERCIAL AND LOGISTICTS LIMITED, a fast growing real estate company with two major brands namely RICHLIFE ESTATE AND GARDENS and RICHLIFE ROYAL CITY with over 500 network of Associates spread across Lagos, other parts of Nigeria and abroad.

He holds a Diploma in Public Accounting and Auditing from Kwara State Polytechnic, Ilorin and BSc in Business Administration from Lagos State University.

He is also a graduate of Leadership Diploma from Word of Faith Bible Institute (WOFBI) and Leadership Certificate from Daystar Leadership Academy (DLA), Lagos.

He is happily married to his lovely wife Helen

www.ingramcontent.com/pod-product-compliance
Lightning Source LLC
Chambersburg PA
CBHW071520220526
45472CB00003B/1089